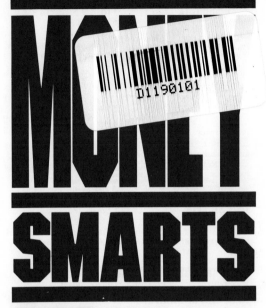

MONEY SMARTS

CONTENTS

Money Smarts

☐ Prevent Medical Overcharges....................1
☐ Buy a Business—with No Money Down............3
☐ College-Tuition Prepayment Plan............6
☐ How to Spot A Forged Check................7
☐ Cheaper Purchase—Protection........................8

Bank Smarts

☐ How to Get A Fair Deal From Your Bank...9
☐ How Safe Is Your Bank?..............................12

☐ FDIC Protection......14
☐ CD Savvy...................15

Investment Smarts

☐ The Darlings of Tax Reform............................16
☐ Safer Investing..........18
☐ Best Time to Invest in Newly Listed Stocks.....18
☐ How to Analyze Corporate Earnings.....19
☐ How to Make A Deal with Your Broker..........21

Insurance Smarts

☐ Unnecessary Insurance Policies........23

☐ Disability Insurance Confidential...................25
☐ Medigap Insurance Trap...............................26
☐ Home Insurance Advice.............................27
☐ Lost Policies Can Be Found............................27

Tax Smarts
☐ Tax Advantages For Filing For Personal Bankruptcy....................28
☐ Profit From Sale-Leaseback.......................31
☐ Tax Reform and Real Estate...............................32
☐ Lowering The Rate On Capital Gains..........34

IRS Smarts
☐ Appealing IRS Audit Conclusions..................35
☐ Quicker Refunds.....38
☐ Don't Pay More Than Necessary.......................38
☐ The IRS Can Track You Down.....................39

Retirement Smarts
☐ Winning Retirement Spots.............................40
☐ Which Pension Plan Payout? 43
☐ Protect Your SS Benefits.............................44
☐ More Deduction From Keoghs & IRAS.............................45
☐ Out-of-State Tax Trap..................................46

Home Smarts
☐ Best Time To Refinance a Mortgage.......................47
☐ Mortgage Sense.......49
☐ The Auction Alternative.....................49
☐ Offering-Price Advice.............................51
☐ Extra-Insurance Protection.......................52
☐ Save on Energy.......53

Travel Smarts
☐ How To Vacation Money-Worry Free.......54
☐ Phone Smarts When Away From Home........56
☐ Ticket-Refund Loophole.......................56
☐ Compensation for Being Bumped..............56
☐ For Emergencies Only...............................57
☐ Get Through US Customs, Cheaply........57
☐ Duty-Free Souvenirs.......................58

Car Smarts
☐ Legally It's a Lemon If........................59
☐ Best Car-Buying Strategy..........................60
☐ Pay Less For Car Insurance......................60
☐ Extended Service— Waste of Money...........61
☐ Tire Trap...................61
☐ Car-Rental Scam.....62

Copyright © 1992 by Boardroom® Reports, Inc.

Printed in the United States of America.

Money Smarts

**PREVENT MEDICAL
OVERCHARGES**

Most people pay very little attention to
the actual fees and expenses charged by
doctors and hospitals. The lenient medical insurance policies of the past (both
private and public) gave people few in-
centives to scrutinize their medical bills.

In the new, more competitive health
care environment, there is a growing
trend by medical insurers toward greater deductibles, less complete insurance
coverage, and copayment policies. The
result is that Americans now have real in-
centives to examine their medical bills
and the appropriateness of individual
charges.

The first step in avoiding overcharges is

1☐

always to ask, ahead of time, what a medical visit, test, or procedure will cost. Don't be shy about asking; if a doctor thinks you can pay the bill, he probably won't bother to volunteer the information. Good health practitioners should present you with a financial estimate along with any plan for major medical work.

Next, negotiate fees or charges. It is absolutely in your best interest to find out all fees and charges involved in your treatment and to negotiate those you feel are too high. Before visiting with a practitioner, find out what and how much your medical insurance plan will cover, and try to negotiate with your doctor any remaining amount. Some doctors will be satisfied with whatever reimbursement your insurance will provide.

The third step in avoiding overcharges: Shop around. It goes against the traditional notion of health care, but you can look for better rates. Fees and hospital charges vary extraordinarily from one practitioner or hospital to another.

Finally, always find out if a test or procedure can be performed on an outpatient basis. Because traditional medical insurance reimbursement policies once favored it, many doctors still routinely admit patients to the hospital for tests or surgery that could be performed on an outpatient basis at a much lower cost.

Source: Arthur A. Levin, MPH, director, Center for Medical Consumers, 237 Thompson St., New York 10012.

BUY A BUSINESS—WITH NO MONEY DOWN

Common dilemma: The owner of a company—call him Mr. Brown—is 65 years old and wants to sell his business. The person best qualified to continue running it (so the company will command a high price) is the general manager—call him Mr. Jones. Jones would like to own the company, but he lacks the cash to buy it.

One solution might be for Jones to try to set up a leveraged buyout. But there are drawbacks:

• The venture will be burdened by collateralized bank loans at high interest rates.

• With heavy loan exposure, banks may be tempted to interfere in the management of the business.

• If Jones has no cash at all, he could wind up with little equity in the company.

From Brown's point of view, the other familiar route to sell his company is through a public offering.

The drawbacks:

• The 1987 stock market crash has made it difficult to raise money by public offerings.

• Red tape of the Securities & Exchange Commission is enormous. Ironically, there are even more SEC restrictions for an established business that wants to go public than for a new one.

New financing options:

Individuals eager to invest in promising companies have set up blind pools. The pools are simply investment funds structured so that the pool takes an equity position in ventures it finances, but members take no management responsibility in the businesses they buy.

Blind pools have been around for a long time, especially in Western mining states. Now they're more popular than ever.

How blind pools work:

Brown wants to sell his XYZ Co. to Jones, the general manager, for $2 million. In a typical deal, Brown would guarantee a $100,000 bank loan for Jones so he can afford a down payment. Brown also signs a letter giving Jones an option to buy the company for $2 million.

Jones takes the letter to a blind pool, which has $200,000 cash and whose stock is traded on the over-the-counter market. If pool management believes the company has a good chance of continued growth and profitability, they can agree to acquire it.

When that happens, they issue new stock in the blind pool so that 85% of the total of the pool is owned by Jones—with 15% ownership remaining with the pool. As part of the transaction, Jones assigns to the pool his right to buy Brown's company.

The $100,000 down payment to Brown comes from the pool. The rest of the pay-

□4

ments made to Brown come from the company's subsequent cash flow and are secured by Jones' stock in the pool.

Moreover, the additional $100,000 that the pool originally had is now available to the company to spend on growth.

What the main players get:

• Brown gets to sell his business at the price he wants to a person he knows can run it. He also gets a stream of payments during his retirement years. He may also receive shares and options for shares in the pool as well as possible consulting agreements.

• Jones gets 85% of the company without using any of his own money.

• Pool members acquire a company worth at least $2 million.

The best way to find blind pools is through lawyers, accountants or brokers who specialize in venture capital and securities matters. If you don't know a professional in one of these fields, ask your own accountant or attorney. He can probably put you in touch with one.

There are currently more than 100 blind pools registered with the Securities & Exchange Commission, but many more are in the process of registering. Most pools are in Colorado and Utah, but also in California, Florida and New York.

Stay away from a blind pool if:

• One or more of its members suggests a side deal, either with the buyer or seller. It's a sign of shady operating.

• There is discussion regarding the stock which implies manipulation that violates SEC law.

Source: Dan Brecher, head of the investment banking department, Bower & Gardner, 110 E. 59 St., New York 10022.

COLLEGE-TUITION PREPAYMENT PLAN

Good news for parents planning to send their children to college: A tuition prepayment plan has been devised that not only would provide a guaranteed hedge against inflation but could be used at any college in the country.

The plan still faces a few hurdles, however. It awaits an OK from the Securities and Exchange Commission (to certify that it's not a security for purposes of investment). . .and the Internal Revenue Service (to agree not to tax the college's earnings on the prepaid funds as an investment).

So far, 18 leading colleges have backed the plan. And there's strong reason to believe that most, if not all, US colleges will adopt the plan after government approval because it would give them a significant recruitment advantage. Critical issues:

• Other pay-now, go-later plans exist, but only on a state-by-state or single-school basis.

• The dollar amount of the installments would be determined by the participating colleges. It would likely be pegged at or near a school's current tuition rates. This would give parents an exact figure to shoot for, rather than estimating what tuitions may be 15 years into the future. If a student opted not to go to a designated college, a prescribed formula would adjust the transfer of payment credits to another school.

• Under the plan, if a student does not attend one of the participating colleges, credit could be transferred to a sibling or even to a first cousin. Failing that, the original investment could be paid back without interest.

For the last decade, college tuition has outpaced inflation by about two percentage points each year. And at least one single-school prepayment plan has been abandoned because of financial difficulties: It could not earn enough on its investment to guarantee future tuition payments without running into the red.

Source: Greg Stringer, president, Hemar Corp., 85 E. 7th Place, educational finance company, St. Paul, MN 55164.

HOW TO SPOT A FORGED CHECK

• See if the check has perforations on one side. (A false check often has four smooth sides, since the forger cuts them with a paper cutter after printing.)
• The code numbers printed on a legitimate check reflect no light. They are printed in magnetic ink, which is dull.
• About 90% of all hot checks are drawn

on accounts less than one year old. The numbers in the upper right-hand corner of the check indicate the age of the account. Be suspicious of those that are numbered 101–150 or 1001–1050 (the starting numbers).

Source: Frank W. Abagnale, once a master forger and now a consultant to banks and retailers, writing in *Real Estate Today*.

CHEAPER PURCHASE-PROTECTION

Credit-card purchase-protection plans are a good deal. It would cost about $13.50 a year to upgrade your insurance policy to get the same no deductible coverage for theft and damage that you get with a purchase on, for instance, a Visa gold card. *Additional savings:* Extended warranties on major purchases would cost an average of $39 per year per item.

Source: Daniel Brigham, Visa USA, Inc., quoted in *USA Today*.

Bank Smarts

HOW TO GET A FAIR DEAL FROM YOUR BANK

Your friendly banker is not your friend. Banks are in business for one reason—to make money. To protect yourself:

• Never buy credit life insurance from a bank. If you die before paying off a bank loan, credit life insurance covers the unpaid balance. The bank receives a hefty fee from the insurance company for selling you the policy—and it relieves itself of a potential collection problem. If you think you need protection, buy the coverage from an insurance company, and save money.

Example: In the case of a 48-month $7,000 loan at 16.79%, credit life insurance from the bank would cost a total of

$380.70 ($275.87 for the policy and $104.83 to finance it). This would cover only the declining balance of the loan as it was paid off. Better: A 35-year-old male can buy $10,000 of life insurance from an insurance company for 48 months for less than $120. He would not only save $260.70 but would also have the full $10,000 of coverage for the entire term of the loan.

• Never buy disability insurance from a bank. If you should be disabled, this insurance covers your loan payments until you are working again.

Example: In the case of a 48-month $7,000 loan at 16.79%, disability insurance from the bank would cost a total of $571.05 ($413.81 for the loan and $157.24 to finance it). You would have to be disabled for almost three out of those 48 months—an unlikely event—to break even.

Trap: By law the bank cannot force you to buy credit life insurance or disability insurance. However, loan officers often present borrowers with contracts that include both policies, but they don't mention to the client that extra costs are involved.

Protection: Have both policies crossed off and initialed by the loan officer on the original contract and on all copies that you sign.

• Don't keep valuables in a safe-deposit box. Safe-deposit boxes can be opened in a few seconds with an ordinary screwdriver. Even the bank vault itself is not burglarproof. And although you can usually replace a marriage license or a birth certificate, the bank's insurance company won't pay you a penny for cash, heirlooms, gold, and other items of value unless you can prove they were in the box. You won't ordinarily be able to do that, because your word (even with backup from others) will be deemed insufficient.

Possible solution: Ask your banker to give you a safekeeping receipt. Drawback: This document must be kept updated, and you will have to reveal the contents of your box to your banker each time you open it.

Better way: Buy your own vault and install it in your home. Then submit a certified list of the vault's contents to your insurance agent. Your homeowner's insurance offers a much greater replacement opportunity than the bank's safe-deposit-box insurance.

Extra protection: It's not hard for the IRS or the state tax authority to get a court order authorizing the opening of your safe-deposit box, and either of them can legally confiscate the contents. If you rent a box, do it at an out-of-town bank where you don't maintain any other accounts. A court order to invade your safe-deposit box is valid only if the location of the box is known.

Source: Edward F. Mrkvicka Jr., president of Reliance Enterprises, a consumer-oriented financial corporation, Box 413, Marengo, IL 60152.

HOW SAFE IS YOUR BANK?

When banks run into financial problems, they behave like any other troubled company. They sometimes try to hide problems and limp along the best they can. For the customer, services can quickly deteriorate. Growing companies can be especially hurt because most rely on their banks to expand credit lines. On the contrary, too often a troubled bank will call in its loans because the bank needs the money—not because the customer is at any growth risk.

Ironically, thousands of customers are unnecessarily hurt. Many could have avoided problems by watching for early-warning signals of bank weakness. Typically, these distress signals show up as early as two years before an outright failure.

Most recent bank problems stem from decisions to grow aggressively. Some banks that failed funded an ambitious growth strategy with "purchased" funds (such as large CDs), as opposed to deposits from their local customer base. That strategy puts them on shaky ground.

Customers that have dealt for some time with banks in this situation usually sense something is wrong:

• There's high turnover among the officers.

• Paperwork and recordkeeping become sloppy.

• The bank encourages customers to extend credit when officers know it really isn't necessary.

But even when customers suspect that a bank is going through some sort of change, they rarely take the trouble to find out if it's merely because of routine personnel problems, for instance, or because of more serious financial trouble.

Essential steps: If a friendly bank officer has recently quit, invite him to lunch and ask him tough questions about his former employer.

If you think there's a problem, get a copy of the bank's Call Report. This twice-a-year document has the data that tell the financial conditions of a bank. (In fact, regardless of whether a customer senses trouble, his finance officer should routinely get Call Reports for banks with which the company does business.)

Although Call Reports are public documents, not all banks make copies available (usually obtainable from the bank's shareholder relations department). But if a bank balks, copies are available from the state agency that regulates banks or from the federal agency under whose jurisdiction it falls (Comptroller of the Currency, Federal Reserve Board of the Federal Deposit Insurance Corp.).

What to look for: By comparing figures of Call Reports over time, a customer can read the warning signals. According to Cates Consulting Analysts, Inc., the signals include:

- Rapid expansion as reflected in a big increase in loan yield relative to other similarly sized banks.
- Loan recovery rate of less than 20%. This is the percentage of written-off bad loans that a bank is ultimately able to recover. It should be well over 20% and is an excellent indication of how riskily the bank is willing to operate.
- Low return on assets for a bank its size (can range from 0.6% for large banks like Citibank and Chase Manhattan to over 1.0% for a small bank).
- High overhead ratio. Failed banks had overhead expenses that amounted to nearly 80% of their income base, compared with a nationwide average of 56%.

FDIC PROTECTION

The dramatic failures of the S&L industry highlight the importance of making full use of deposit insurance provided by the Federal Deposit Insurance Corporation (FDIC). Rules:
- The FDIC insures up to $100,000 of an individual's total deposits at any one institution. Thus, if you have a checking account, savings account and certificate of deposit at one bank, the $100,000 limit applies to your combined balance.
- The limit applies separately to accounts in different banks, so you can multiply protection by keeping accounts in more than one bank.

• Your $100,000 of insurance will cover your share of joint accounts held in any one institution. (The bank will assume your share is equal to that of the other account owners unless told otherwise.)

• With joint accounts, opening an account of a different type (such as an IRA or Keogh) can give you $100,000 of extra coverage for each different type of account.

Source: Don Inscoe, chief banking analyst, Veribanc, Box 461, Wakefield, MA 01880.

CD SAVVY

• Buy several certificates of deposit (CDs) in small denominations instead of one large one. Reason: If you need only part of the money, you won't have to withdraw it all and pay an early withdrawal penalty on the full amount.

• When setting up an out-of-state certificate of deposit account, get the name of the bank officer you are working with . . . verify the terms of the CD account . . . and ask the officer to assign you an account number. When you send the deposit check, make it payable to the account number.

Source: William Donoghue, chairman, The Donoghue Organization, Holliston, MA.

Investment Smarts

THE DARLINGS OF TAX REFORM

Deferred annuities can serve as an alternative for individuals whose incentive to continue to make IRA contributions was greatly weakened by tax reform. Although contributions to a deferred annuity are not tax deductible, earnings do accumulate tax deferred. Advantage over an IRA: There is no limit to the amount of money you can invest in an annuity.

The new variable annuity can serve as the ideal replacement for investments that used to receive the benefit of favorable long-term capital gains treatment. Long-term gains from investments in stocks can be sheltered in a variable annuity. That income is not taxed until you withdraw your money.

□16

How annuities work: An individual buys an annuity from an insurance company, paying a lump sum or a series of payments over time. In return, the insurance company guarantees that the funds will grow at a certain tax-free rate. Then, beginning on a specified date, the individual receives regular income payments for life.

Payments depend on the amount of money contributed to the account, the length of time the funds are left in it, and the rate of return earned on the funds. Also a factor in determining the size of the payments is whether you include your spouse and other heirs as beneficiaries. Different options enable you to have payments continue to your spouse, or to your children, or for a minimum of, say, 20 years, regardless of who is there to receive them after you die.

Deferred annuities therefore can be considered part insurance and part investment. If you are willing to part with at least $5,000 (the minimum amount can differ from company to company) for five years or longer, you can be guaranteed a competitive, tax-free return on your funds. Because the earned income is not taxed until you begin withdrawing the money (presumably at a lower tax rate), your funds accumulate much faster than they would if they were taxed. The insurance component, of course, is guaranteed regular monthly income payments for the rest of your life—taking the worry and risk out of budgeting for your retirement income. Also, should you die before you begin receiving payments, your heirs are guaranteed to receive the full amount of your original principal.

Source: Alexandra Armstrong, Alexandra Armstrong Advisors, Inc., 1140 Connecticut Ave. NW, Washington, DC 20036.

SAFER INVESTING

Municipal bonds are safer than most investments, but they're not risk-free. You can't rely on national credit rating services. By the time they downgrade a bond, it has usually depreciated. Moreover, the services may not follow all issues. Protection: Invest in a mutual fund. All leading fund groups do credit analysis and make their own changes in ratings well before the published changes.

BEST TIME TO INVEST IN NEWLY LISTED STOCKS

Most investors believe that a stock will rise in price as soon as it moves from an over-the-counter listing to the New York Stock Exchange. That's rarely true. What happens:

The prices of such shares tend to run up sharply on the smaller exchange in the year preceding the NYSE listing. Foreknowledge of listings may or may not be available to shareholders, however, and you can't necessarily presume that you'll benefit from this information.

During the average nine-week period required for the NYSE to consider applications for listing, stocks that move from the over-the-counter markets usually outperform other stocks. If you hold such an issue, keep it until the listing procedure is completed.

Once listing has been achieved, expect the price performance of such issues to fall to below average. Weakness is usually particularly acute during the first six weeks following listing, and this weakness can linger for as long as a year.

Hold or buy as soon as applications for an NYSE listing are made, but plan to sell when the application is approved. Be careful: A few issues will rise in price even after listing is complete, and some will fall during the periods just prior to listing.

Source: *Market Logic.*

HOW TO ANALYZE CORPORATE EARNINGS

There are ways that a dedicated investor who's willing to do some serious work can get an edge on the market. That's by looking for significant data in the financial reports that managements issue each quarter. Many professionals overlook the early warning signs that are revealed in corporate shareholder reports.

The fundamentals to check in every earnings report:

• A bulge in accounts payable. The company may be short of cash and stretching out bill payments. Watch out!

• Short-term debt. Look carefully at this because many companies are covering up short-term liabilities (such as commercial paper) and calling it longer-term debt since it's covered by a bank's line of credit. Short-term debt is a burden on a company, making it vulnerable to interest rate increases. Also, the company's bankers may force the company to amend loan covenants, curtailing the operating flexibility of the company in a way that can be detrimental to the long-term interest of all the present shareholders.

• Dividend payout. Too many managements are unwilling to cut dividends during tough strikes or other sharp reverses. When a company's resources are drained to pay a dividend, start worrying about the quality of management. It takes tough managers to cut a dividend. And, in the long run, tough managers are usually very good to shareholders.

• One of the most bullish signs in an earnings report is a big bath—a big writeoff, often associated with a long overdue restructuring of operations, including the sale of losing or low-margined businesses. Among the classic examples: Beatrice Foods, Gulf & Western, and Ralston Purina. Chances are good, with a big bath, for a real turnaround in earnings. Wall Street may be disappointed at first, but it usually reads a big bath positively and increases the price/earnings multiple on the stock.

Source: Ted O'glove, author of *The Quality of Earnings Report*, published by Reporting Research Corp., Englewood Cliffs, NJ.

HOW TO MAKE A DEAL WITH YOUR BROKER

So-called standard rates are almost always negotiable. If you like your stockbroker but want to pay lower commissions and interest rates here's what to do:

• Check the ads in *Baron's* or call a couple of discount brokers for their rate structures. Once you have the facts, visit your broker and explain that other brokers charge much less than he does, and that you'd like to discuss a new, fairer arrangement.

• Show your proof (ads or notes you took while calling discounters). Expect the usual responses about excellent service, discounts that depend on volume, your account is too small, etc. Your response: "My account doesn't require much servicing. I don't use your research or other expensive facilities and I'm not asking for the moon. I just don't think it's fair that I have to pay the top rate."

• If the broker says that he can't help you, ask him who can. Inside information: After running my own Wall St. firm, I know that the broker probably has more discretion than he's willing to disclose. He should be able to arrange a 20%–30% discount off the top rate.

• That accomplished, ask for one last favor: You're paying the firm's highest interest rate on your debit balance, and you'd like a one-percentage-point discount. Since brokers usually charge one-half to two percentage points above prime, a one-point reduction off the high end of this gravy isn't unreasonable . . . even for a small account. If you're told that rates are based on the size of the debit balance, explain that you know rates are negotiable, that others pay less and that you'd like the same treatment as those paying less.

• Later: Negotiate for your share of free stock guides and charts, access to the broker's financial library and occasional shares of "hot" issues.

You have a right to these, but you won't be handed them on a silver platter. You have to ask for them.

Source: Ralph Charell, CEO of his own Wall St. securities firm and former TV programming executive.

Insurance Smarts

UNNECESSARY INSURANCE POLICIES

The best rule when purchasing insurance: Buy only comprehensive policies that will protect you against all catastrophic economic eventualities in a particular category.

Piecemeal policies leave gaps in coverage. After years of paying premiums, you get absolutely nothing if your accident or illness falls between the policies' provisions. In addition, piecemeal coverage is always more expensive than comprehensive coverage.

Policies to avoid:

• Cancer insurance. If you wind up in a hospital or bedridden at home, you'll want to collect for any disease.

• Air-travel life insurance. Fear of flying aside, this is a terrible deal statistically. If you have a dependent, you need good life insurance to cover any cause of death. Besides, your survivors can sue an airline.

• Accident life insurance. Will your survivors need more money if you die in an accident rather than from natural causes?

• Automobile medical insurance. Your comprehensive health plan will cover your medical expenses, while auto liability coverage will take care of your passengers.

• Rental-car insurance. When you had to assume only a $500 deductible, this was easy to ignore. Now that the deductible is commonly $3,000, it's a tougher call. But before you fork over an exorbitant $7 a day (to cover liability and physical damage to the car), call your agent. Your current auto policy may already cover cars you rent.

• Credit insurance. This policy pays off loans in the event of your death—for a usurious fee. Example: A three-year policy on a $5,000 loan costs $144 in annual premiums. . .for average coverage of only $2,500. (Coverage decreases as the loan is repaid.) But a 40-year-old man can buy $250,000 in annual renewable term life insurance for $350 a year—100 times the coverage for less than triple the premium.

• Mortgage insurance. Again, annual renewable term is a superior deal. With mortgage policies, your coverage slides as your debt declines. With term life insurance, your coverage is constant—unless you choose to reduce it to cut your premiums.

Source: Bob Hunter, president, National Insurance Consumer Organization, 121 N. Payne St., Alexandria, VA 22314.

DISABILITY INSURANCE CONFIDENTIAL

When disability strikes, you have to replace your income with something or face losing your house, your lifestyle, savings and investments. Ironically, most people routinely buy life insurance to protect their families in case they die, but they neglect to buy disability insurance. Fact: Chances of being disabled during your working years are four to five times greater than chances of dying during the same period.

Comparing policies:

Concern #1: How the policy defines disability. You want the broadest definition you can find and/or afford. Some policies, for example, define disability as inability to perform any of the duties required by your occupation. Be careful: Under many definitions, including that of Social Security, disability is the inability to perform any occupation. Under that definition, you get no payment as long as you can work at something, even if the job you can perform after being disabled is low paying.

A split definition of disability that's often used: Strict for a specific period of time and broad for the duration of the benefit period.

Concern #2: The length of the benefit period. Will the policy continue to pay you after age 65? Many policies stop paying then and you may still need funds. Unless another retirement fund kicks in, you'd have an income gap.

Also: Check the waiting period, the time between the start of the disability and the actual beginning of payment of benefits. If you can wait 90 days before you need income, the premiums will be significantly lower than if you wait only 30 days.

Example: A person who is 45 years old wants a disability policy that will protect his income of $55,000 a year. Yearly premiums with a 30-day waiting period will cost $1,900—with a 60-day wait, $1,700—and for a 90-day waiting period, $1,550.

Source: Karen P. Schaeffer, Schaeffer Financial, Greenbelt, MD.

MEDIGAP INSURANCE TRAP

Many medigap policies, offered to cover expenses not covered by medicare, are a very bad buy. A study by the United States General Accounting Office found that most medigap policies pay out less than 60 cents of benefits for every dollar of premiums collected. Some of the policies were found to pay out one cent per premium dollar. Important: Shop around aggressively and examine medigap policy coverage carefully.

HOME INSURANCE ADVICE

Be sure to insure your home for its replacement cost rather than its market value. The two may not be the same. For example, while the neighborhood might have a big impact on a house's market value, it shouldn't have a big impact on construction costs if the house should ever have to be rebuilt.

Source: Janice M. Johnson, partner, BDO Seidman, 15 Columbus Circle, New York 10023.

LOST POLICIES CAN BE FOUND

Lost insurance policies can often be located through the American Council of Life Insurance (ACLI). Procedure: Write the ACLI for a policy-search questionnaire (include a stamped, self-addressed business-size envelope) . . . fill out and return the form to ACLI, which will forward the information to the 100-or-so insurance companies participating in the missing-policy service. If one of these companies holds the policy, a company representative will contact you.

Source: ACLI, 1001 Pennsylvania Ave. NW, Washington, DC 20004.

Tax Smarts

TAX ADVANTAGES FOR FILING
FOR PERSONAL BANKRUPTCY

Tax considerations are hardly ever the main reason an individual files for bankruptcy. But the tax aspects of personal bankruptcy can be very favorable, especially for taxpayers who are heavily in debt to their employers or to their own closely held corporations. Main benefits:

• Cancellation of indebtedness. As a general rule, when a debt is forgiven, the debtor must report the amount forgiven as income. But a debt cancelled in bankruptcy is not treated as income.

Example: Among other debts, a financially troubled taxpayer owes his employer $25,000. If the debt is simply forgiven by the employer, the employee must report the $25,000 as income. If, however, the employee files for bankruptcy and the debt is cancelled, he does not have to treat it as income.

Example: An individual had credit card charges of $10,000 last year. This year the credit card debt is discharged in bankruptcy. If any of the credit card charges were previously deducted (e.g., as a business entertainment deduction) they would have to be reported as income. But the other part of the discharged debt wouldn't have to be reported.

Example: Five years ago, an individual borrowed heavily from his closely held corporation. For other reasons business is now so bad that the corporation must file for bankruptcy. If the individual also declares bankruptcy and the loan is discharged, he has a big tax windfall. He will not have to pick up the money he borrowed from the company as income.

• Cancellation of back taxes. Unpaid federal income taxes are cancelled in bankruptcy if they become due more than three years before the bankruptcy filing.

• Deductible expenses. Fees paid to an accountant to prepare an individual's personal records for Bankruptcy Court are tax deductible. So are legal fees, to the extent they involve the tax aspects of bankruptcy.

• Carryovers. Some carryovers are retained by the individual after bankruptcy. Included: Net operating loss carryovers (business losses), capital loss carryovers, tax credit carryovers and charitable contribution carryovers. Limit: Net operating loss carryovers must be adjusted downward to the extent that the debt giving rise to the carryovers is cancelled in bankruptcy.

The negative tax consequences of personal bankruptcy:

• Recapture of credits. Any investment credit taken on an asset that is disposed of in the course of the bankruptcy proceeding must be recaptured (that is, added back to the tax due on the individual's post-bankruptcy tax return).

• Payroll taxes. Individuals who are personally responsible for payroll taxes (e.g., officers of a company) cannot cancel their liability for those taxes in bankruptcy.

• Tax refunds are payable to the trustee in bankruptcy, not to the individual who files for bankruptcy. Loophole: Taxpayers who expect to file for bankruptcy next year should arrange payroll withholding this year so that no tax refunds will be coming from the government. Alternative: If large refunds are expected, file for bankruptcy prior to December 31, before the refund becomes an asset payable to the bankruptcy trustee.

Source: Edward Mendlowitz, partner, Mendlowitz Weitsen, CPAs, Two Penn Plaza, New York 10121.

PROFIT FROM SALE-LEASEBACK

You can create significant income and estate tax savings by buying your parents'
home and renting it back to them. Sale-
leasebacks, as these transactions are com-
monly known, enable taxpayers to sell a
dwelling unit to a family member and
then lease it back from the buyer. If your
parents are 55 or over, the Tax Code will
permit an exclusion of up to $125,000
profit from the sale of the dwelling.

Advantages of a sale-leaseback:
• Future appreciation of the house is no
longer included in the parents' estate.
• You can shelter income by deducting
depreciation and the expenses of owning
and maintaining the dwelling.
• Your parents can receive cash in exchange for the equity value of their home.
• Your parents can utilize the one-time
$125,000 exclusion on the gain from the
sale of their residence.
• Your parents enjoy the advantages of
renting while remaining in the family
home (i.e., they are no longer responsible
for maintaining the property).

The most appropriate candidates for
this type of arrangement are parents who
have only modest savings and income but
own a home with a significant amount of
equity value locked up in it. A sale-
leaseback is especially appropriate for
parents who rely on their children for a
portion of their income, since the sale's

proceeds give them a steady source of additional cash.

For a sale-leaseback to be considered valid, the following conditions must be met:
• The home must be purchased for adequate and full consideration.
• You as the buyer must bear the risks and the benefits of fluctuations in the residential real estate market.
• Your parents must be subject to lease provisions.
• There must be no evidence of intention by your parents to repurchase the property.
• Your parents must not retain control over the property or exercise dominion and control over you.
• You must collect a "fair rent" from your parents.

Source: Israel A. Press, CPA, tax partner, and Tom Spiesman, JD, tax associate, Touche Ross & Company, Financial Services Center, One World Trade Center, New York 10048.

TAX REFORM AND REAL ESTATE

Under tax reform there are still many ways for individuals to use real estate to cut their tax bills. Ideas:
• While tax reform doesn't let you currently deduct real estate losses from salary or investment income, it does let you carry such losses forward to future years to offset future gains from real estate. Thus, if you own property that's appreciating in value, it may pay to hold it for a

few years, then sell it and use your accumulated losses to shelter your gain from tax.

• If you own your own business, you can retain personal ownership of real estate used by the business, then have the business lease the property from you. Advantages: You can set the terms of the lease (though it must provide for a rent that's reasonable in relation to the market). Thus, you can fix the lease to provide you with income that will be sheltered from tax by losses you're receiving from other investments. Or the lease can provide losses that you can use to shelter your other investment income.

• Under a special provision of tax reform, those with income of under $100,000 can still make direct investments in real estate and deduct up to $25,000 in losses each year. Thus, a person can buy an apartment or house, rent it out and use the tax losses that result to cut the taxes owed on salary or investment income. Requirements: You must own the property directly, not as an investor in a limited partnership. And you must actively manage the investment property yourself.

Future investments:

The market for real estate investments is as active as ever after tax reform, but expect dramatic changes in the way these deals are packaged and sold. Look for income deals. Most attractive under the new law is real estate deals that are structured to produce annual cash flow for the investor. Because depreciation deductions remain large under the new law, this income can be sheltered from tax, with excess depreciation being accumulated to shelter ultimate gain when the property is sold. Result: The investor receives tax-free income similar to that which might be obtained from an investment in tax-exempt bonds—with a chance for additional large profits through the property's appreciation.

Source: Glenn Davis, partner, Seidman & Seidman/BDO, 15 Columbus Circle, New York 10023.

LOWERING THE RATE ON CAPITAL GAINS

Give appreciated securities to your parents instead of cash if you are supporting them. They can cash in the securities and pay tax on the appreciation in their low tax bracket. You'll avoid paying tax in your high tax bracket. Caution: A large gain could push your parents into a higher bracket.

IRS Smarts

APPEALING IRS AUDIT CONCLUSIONS

The best forum to fight in, after the audit or examiner level, is the IRS's own Appellate Division. There, taxpayers who disagree with IRS audit conclusions and who can document their position with sound facts have a good chance of getting at least part of what they're asking for, without going to court.

An appeal to the appellate level of the IRS is handled by highly trained IRS personnel called appeals officers. It is the appeals officers' job to settle cases, to see that they don't go to court, while still getting the most they can for the government.

Unlike auditors, who are bound by the regulations and rulings of the IRS, the appeals officer is entitled to consider the hazards of litigation. That is, the chance that the government might lose in court if it litigates a case. If the officer feels that the government has a weak position on the facts, or there are cases in the taxpayer's jurisdiction against the government, odds are that he will concede or agree to a settlement.

The officer has a great deal of leeway. It is possible for a taxpayer to horse-trade and negotiate on individual items with conferees. Typical is for the officer to concede half the tax bill (or a third of the bill) as being deductible. The taxpayer will have to concede the other half or two-thirds.

Some issues that are not likely to be settled at the audit level, but which taxpayers have a good chance of resolving at appeal, are:

• Cash expenditures that the auditor has disallowed for lack of documentation where those expenditures are common in the taxpayer's business.

• Travel and entertainment deductions that are disallowed because the taxpayer does not have all the support the tax law requires. These disallowances can normally be settled on appeal if the amounts are reasonable.

• Business use of property. A taxpayer uses his car in business 75% of the time, say. But the auditor says he hasn't supported his deduction. If the taxpayer can show that he normally uses his car in business, an appeal should be successful.

• Charitable contributions. Large deductions and those involving hard-to-value gifts, such as stock in a closely held business, become battles of appraisals. These often need to be settled on appeal.

• Constructive dividends. Are items of expense paid by a closely held company to an officer-shareholder deductible, or are they a nondeductible preferential dividend?

But do not go up through the appeal process on a lark, hoping for the best outcome. Prepare a decent case. Get sound professional advice. The appeals officers are technically competent people. They are not likely to let anything slip by them.

Do not expect to get 100% of what you ask for. If several issues are taken to appeal, be prepared to concede some as part of the give-and-take negotiations.

Cases that involve questions of fact rather than law have the best chance of being settled because facts lend themselves to compromise. On legal issues, there's room for negotiation. For every six cases the taxpayer can come up with in support of a legal position, the appeals officer will have six for the government. There's a standoff, which the officer will have no choice but to resolve on the principal of hazards of litigation.

The best approach in dealing with an appeals officer (or an auditor, for that matter) is to give as much factual background as possible. Point out where the auditor was wrong. Support that position with facts. What prevails is a strong factual presentation, forcefully argued.

Source: David E. Lipson, partner in charge of the tax division of the Chicago office of Arthur Andersen & Co.

QUICKER REFUNDS

Tax-refund checks can now be issued much faster. Time has been cut from six weeks to two weeks. . .and the refund may now be deposited directly into a taxpayer's bank account—if you file through a professional tax preparer who uses IRS-sanctioned software to tie into the IRS's electronic filing system.

Source: *Personal Computing*, 10 Holland Dr., Hasbrouck Heights, NJ 07604.

DON'T PAY MORE THAN NECESSARY

Suppose you owe the IRS $10,000 for 1990 taxes, but the IRS owes you $2,000 from 1989. Must you pay the $10,000 first and then wait for a refund? Absolutely not! You have every right to pay only the net amount—$8,000. Don't let a revenue officer pressure you into paying more. The revenue officer simply wants to close the case in a hurry and doesn't want to wait for the service center to process your refund. Even though the officer may threaten to seize your assets or levy your salary if you don't pay the gross amount owed, you should continue to offer to pay only the net amount. Tip: If the pressure gets hard to handle, ask to meet with the officer's group manager or branch chief. Bring a check with you for the net amount owed.

Source: Ms. X is a former IRS agent, still well-connected.

THE IRS CAN TRACK YOU DOWN

How does the IRS find people who owe them money and have skipped town? Revenue officers are instructed to interview neighbors, school officials, former employers and fellow employees in an effort to find a taxpayer's whereabouts. Here are some of the contacts that may provide clues:

• Neighbors may know where the taxpayer moved.
• A former landlord may have a rental application which could reveal leads.
• School officials may know where children's records have been transferred.
• A former employer may have been called as a job reference from a new employer in a new town.
• Utility companies may have a new address where a security deposit was mailed.
• The Post Office may have been supplied with a forwarding address.

Source: Ms. X is a former IRS agent, still well-connected.

Retirement Smarts

WINNING RETIREMENT SPOTS

Many of us hope that snow shovels, galoshes, and earmuffs will be things of the past when we reach our "golden" years. And unless you're one of those hearty individuals who can't wait for the first nip of frost, a white Christmas, and delicious, sweet sap running from the maples, you're probably dreaming that your magic retirement address will be somewhere in the Sun Belt. But instead of following the crowd, you may be hoping to find a more private haven.

Using a combination of standards—including cost of living, crime rate, temperature and humidity, air quality, housing, medical facilities, and cultural and recreational activities—we arrived at the leading candidates. Here are a few of them:

Tryon, North Carolina:

This little city, population 4,000, is called Shangri-La by some of its residents. It's in the western end of the state, in the Appalachian Highlands. But don't assume it's in the sticks, just because it's off the beaten track. About half its residents are retired, sophisticated people from all parts of the US and the world, representing both business and the arts. Its Fine Arts Center is home to theater, art, music, and films.

One feature that attracts people to Tryon is its weather. It's in a thermal belt that makes its weather uniquely comfortable year-round. With mountains to the north and east, it's sheltered from the cold. But since it's exposed to the south, warm air swaddles the area in a temperature inversion that keeps the temperature relatively stable from summer to winter. Sun is plentiful, making it a gardener's delight, with the growing season lasting about 200 days. That creates an abundance of fresh farm and orchard produce.

Sports facilities are abundant, too: Well-lighted tennis courts, a year-round swim club, two golf courses, horseback riding, hiking, and even special "enrichment centers" that provide game and craft activities for retired residents.

Housing is more than adequate. Medical facilities are also good, and comparatively inexpensive.

Jekyll Island, Georgia:

This community is one of the three so-called Golden Isles off the Georgia coast. State-owned Jekyll Island has only about 1,200 residents. It used to be a retreat where the Rockefellers, Morgans, Goulds, and Vanderbilts built "cottages." Although the island has been converted into a public park, private homes are available under an unusual arrangement: You can buy a house, but the land upon which it sits must be rented (on a 99-year lease) from the state.

The weather is moderate. And although the island occasionally has snow, it's not unusual to eat Christmas dinner outdoors in shirtsleeves.

Medical facilities in Brunswick are superior. Living costs are moderate. If you fish for your supper, which many do, and frequent the local farm stands, grocery bills will be even lower.

Covington, Louisiana:

This lovely town (population 8,000) is only a half-hour ride from New Orleans and right in the middle of the so-called Ozone Belt (a pine-covered section north of Lake Pontchartrain, considered by many to be one of the world's most healthful regions). The land is above sea level and remains cooler than New Orleans in the summer. Although winters are mild, there are occasional cold snaps with snow. The mean temperature in January is 55°, in July, 80°. Autumn days have the crispness of New England, and the leaves turn orange and gold.

Home prices range widely. Medical facilities here are exceptionally good, and the area has a well-rounded cultural program, independent of nearby New Orleans.

Roswell, New Mexico:

In the middle of the state's retirement center, Roswell has a population of 50,000. Summer temperatures average 77°, with low humidity (30% in the midafternoon). Nighttime temperatures often drop to freezing, but since the sun shines 70% of the time, the days warm up quickly. In this wide-open country you can drive for hours without seeing a house. Roswell is the largest town in the area, an urban oasis in the desert.

Although the town has the best medical facilities in the area, they are not quite as good as those of the other areas mentioned. Housing is inexpensive. Cultural activities include a symphony orchestra and a little theater.

Source: Peter A. Dickinson, author of *Sunbelt Retirement*, a survey of the best cities in the Sun Belt to consider for retirement.

WHICH PENSION PLAN PAYOUT?

Key retirement planning decision: Which method of tax-cutting income averaging should be applied to a lump-sum payment from a company retirement plan? They're available to persons who reached age 50 before January 1, 1986, when Tax Reform became effective.

Choice: The old law's 10-year income-averaging method, or Tax Reform's new five-year method. The 10-year method is still best for most payouts, but large distributions may be subject to less tax under the five-year method because of Tax Reform's lower top tax rate. Breakeven point: A payout of $473,000. Get the advice of a tax expert before deciding how to take any pension plan payout.

Source: The Wyatt Company, 303 West Madison, Chicago 60606.

PROTECT YOUR SS BENEFITS

Your Social Security benefits are taxable if your total income for the year exceeds these dollar limits:

• $25,000, if you are single.

• $32,000, if you are married and file a joint return.

• $25,000, if you are married, do not file a joint return. . .and do not live with your spouse.

• Zero if you are married, do not file a joint return, and did live with your spouse at any time during the year.

Trap: Total income includes tax-exempt income, such as interest received from municipal bonds, which is free of income tax. If you are likely to exceed the income limits, consider these following strategies:

• Invest in assets that appreciate in value without producing current income—essentially Series EE savings bonds or growth stocks. Such investments can help keep you under the income limit.

• Time that income (IRA withdrawals, etc.) so that you receive it advantageously, such as when you have offsetting deductible expenses.

• Divorce. While a married couple filing jointly will have a $32,000 income limit, two single people can take $25,000 each, or $50,000 together.

MORE DEDUCTION FROM KEOGHS & IRAS

A contribution to your Keogh plan, IRA, or company 401(k) plan not only gives you the benefit of a tax deduction, it may also increase *other* deductions you claim, and cut your state and local tax bills as well. Key: The contribution cuts your Adjusted Gross Income, which limits several other deductions...

• Miscellaneous expenses are deductible to the extent that they exceed 2% of AGI.

• Medical costs are deductible to the extent that they exceed 7.5% of AGI.

• Casualty losses are deductible to the extent that they exceed 10% of AGI.

Moreover, many states and localities

base their tax bills on federal AGI.

Example: A person contributes $7,000 to his company 401(k). He not only gets the benefit of a $7,000 deduction, but any miscellaneous expense deduction he claims will *also* be increased by $140, any medical deduction by $525, and any casualty loss deduction by $700. And state and local taxes may be cut as well.

Add in the fact that investment earnings which accrue in a retirement account are tax-deferred, and you can see that a retirement plan contribution may be your very best tax shelter.

Source: Pamela Pecarich, partner, and Steven Woolf, tax manager, office of national tax services, Coopers & Lybrand, 1800 M St. NW, Washington, DC 20036.

OUT-OF-STATE TAX TRAP

Retirees who relocate may find that their pensions remain taxable in the state they've moved from. Examples: California and New Jersey take income tax on pension benefits regardless of the recipient's current residence. Rationale: Pension benefits were accrued during working years, and income earned in a particular state should be taxed in that state. Two bills have been proposed in Congress to end this practice.

Source: *Medical Economics*, 680 Kinderkamack Rd., Oradell, NJ 07649.

Home Smarts

BEST TIME TO REFINANCE A MORTGAGE

The most common type of mortgage is the conventional credit agreement for a fixed-rate, self-amortizing loan. Since each periodic payment is a fixed amount for each installment, the division between principal and interest will change constantly. In the early years almost all of the payment will cover interest costs. As time goes on, the principal is repaid, the proportion changes. There will eventually come a point where most of the payment will be applied to principal.

Since the interest expense is deductible, the early period of a fixed-rate, self-amortizing loan provides a larger tax deduction. Therefore, most real estate investors prefer to refinance a loan at the point where principal repayments become a major portion of the installment payment. Below is a table setting forth the percentage of loan principal remaining for various interest rates and maturities of loans. The percent equity buildup in a particular mortgage will be the difference between the loan principal remaining and 100 percent.

			Loan Remaining After			
Interest rate	5 years	10 years	15 years	20 years	25 years	30 years
			Life of mortgage—30 years			
7%	94%	86%	74%	57%	33%	0%
7½	95	87	75	59	34	0
8	95	88	77	60	36	0
9	96	89	79	63	39	0
10	97	91	82	66	41	0
			Life of mortgage—25 years			
7%	91%	79%	61%	36%	0%	
7½	92	80	62	37	0	
8	92	81	64	38	0	
9	93	83	66	40	0	
10	94	85	69	43	0	
			Life of mortgage—20 years			
7%	86%	67%	39%	0%		
7½	87	68	40	0		
8	87	79	41	0		
9	89	71	43	0		
10	90	73	45	0		

Source: *How to Make Money in Real Estate*, Steven James Lee, Boardroom Books, Springfield, NJ.

MORTGAGE $ENSE

Advantages of loan assumption (taking over an existing mortgage) when buying a home: Small assumption fee (about $50), instead of paying several points to obtain a new loan. . .a lower-than-market interest rate, thus a lower monthly payment. . .no qualification required—you do not need to have good credit. . .the loan you assume is assumable by the next buyer, making the property more salable. Note: Not all mortgages are assumable—check the mortgage contract.

Source: *The Ultimate Guide to Residential Real Estate Loans* by Andrew James McLean, John Wiley & Sons, 605 Third Ave., New York 10158.

THE AUCTION ALTERNATIVE

In today's tight real-estate market, many people are turning to auctions to generate the interest needed to sell their homes. An auction is a quick and efficient way to sell a house, a condo, even acreage, with *no* contingencies. Auction buyers are solid buyers, so financing is rarely a problem. Virtually 100% of auction contracts close.

To sell your property at auction:

• Contact a professional auctioneer who has experience selling property similar to yours. The National Auctioneers Association publishes a national directory of auctioneers. Questions to ask:

1. Will you do target-market research to determine what kind of customer my

property should be promoted to?

2. Are you willing to share your commission with local real-estate brokers to get the benefit of their advertising?

3. Will you purchase the mailing lists needed to attract the proper prospects?

• The auctioneer inspects your property and sets a timetable and fees. It usually takes about 45 days to advertise and set up the auction.

Costs: In most cases, you will be asked to pay 1%–4% of the appraised value of your home to cover advertising expenses. In addition, you must pay a commission of 5%–10% to the auctioneer. A portion would be shared with the broker whose client buys the property.

• You decide what kind of auction to hold. There are two types:

1. Absolute. The property sells to the highest bidder, period.

2. Subject to confirmation. The seller establishes a minimum price that he/she will accept for the property.

Although the second choice sounds more beneficial to the buyer, the first generates more interest, because people love a potential bargain. Benefit: The more interest you get, the hotter the auction. Sometimes the price is driven higher than what you would get in a subject to confirmation auction.

• The listing agreement is discussed and signed. This is similar to the listing agreement you would sign with a traditional broker.

• A sign is put on your property to promote the auction. In addition, ads are placed in local papers and a brochure describing your property is distributed to prospective buyers.

• A preview of your home is scheduled before the auction. On this date, prospective buyers can inspect your property.

Because everyone comes on the same day, an auction generates more enthusiasm for and competition over your property. This also enables you to maintain some privacy while your home is on the market—you won't have brokers bringing people through at all hours.

• Another preview is held the day of the auction. This gives interested buyers a last chance to look over the property before the bidding begins.

• The auction takes place at your home. Prospective buyers bring cash or a cashier's check, the amount of which is designated in your listing agreement and is nonrefundable if financing falls through. The buyer then has 45 to 60 days to close on the property.

Source: Jim Gall, chairman of the board and founder of Auction Company of America, 100 N. Biscayne Blvd., Miami 33132.

OFFERING-PRICE ADVICE

When bidding to buy a new home, most

buyers think the first offer should be 10%–15% below the asking price. Better: Adapt bidding to the buying conditions. Ask:

• How is the local real-estate market? If it's stagnant, an offer *more than* 15% below the asking price may be reasonable. If homes are selling quickly, a low offer won't be considered.

• Is the asking price already a good value? The owner may need to sell fast.

• How long has the house been for sale? The longer it has been on the market, the greater the bidder's bargaining power. A low offer is less likely to succeed if the house is new to the market.

Source: Survey of real-estate experts, published in *Medical Economics*, 680 Kinderkamack Rd., Oradell, NJ 07649.

EXTRA-INSURANCE PROTECTION

Homeowners' insurance policies typically pay only 10% of the insured value of items that were taken out of the home (such as a computer taken by a child to college which was stolen or lost). Also, while homeowners' policies do cover fire and theft, they do not cover damage from power surges, which can damage valuable electrical equipment. Solution: A valuable-items floater added to your homeowners' policy. Cost: About 75¢ per $100 of coverage.

SAVE ON ENERGY

• The cooling effects of a big tree can save an urban homeowner $73 a year in air-conditioning bills. Bottom line: 100 million trees would save American homeowners and businesses more than $4 billion annually in energy bills.

Source: *World Watch*, 1776 Massachusetts Ave. NW, Washington, DC 20036.

• Turn your heat down 10 degrees for eight hours at night, and you'll cut your annual heating bill roughly 11%. Turn it down for eight hours at night and eight hours during the day and you will save 22%. If that's too cold: Turning it down only five degrees for two eight-hour periods a day will still save you 15% annually.

Source: Field tests and computer simulations by Honeywell, Inc., reported in *Harrowsmith*, The Creamery, Charlotte, VT 05445.

Travel Smarts

HOW TO VACATION
MONEY-WORRY FREE

To be financially worry-free during a travel vacation—what to do before you leave:

• Get your bank's list of automatic teller machine networks. Reason: In some foreign countries, you can use your ATM card or credit card to get local currency without paying a foreign-exchange commission.

• Buy traveler's cheques—they are safer than carrying cash. Deposit cheques left over as soon as you return so you can resume building interest.

• Check your own car-insurance policy. Many plans cover non-business use of another car. . .which means you can save money by declining the damage waiver on a rental.

• Set money aside to get a head-start paying charges you accumulate on credit cards during your trip.

• Use a travel agent—they help you compare vacation spots and make arrangements easier.

• Copy front and back of all credit cards. Take a copy with you and keep another at home. Reason: You can give information quickly and accurately to credit-card companies in case cards are stolen or lost.

• Decide how much money you can afford to spend on souvenirs and gifts. . . and stick to that amount.

During the trip:

• Don't keep cash or valuables in checked luggage. . .or in hotel rooms. Carry them on planes and use hotel safes. Don't hang cash-containing purses on one shoulder —strap them across your body.

• Exchange American money for foreign currency at banks—you'll get better rates there than at airports and hotels. Exchange foreign coins before leaving the country you visited—US banks only exchange paper money.

• Have money left for take-out meals or dining out upon your return from vacation. Return one day before going back to work in order to be well rested.

Source: Credit Union National Association.

PHONE SMARTS WHEN AWAY FROM HOME

• Take advantage of free local calls that can be made from many VIP lounges at major airports.

• Don't charge in-state calls to a hotel room. A hotel usually adds a service charge to them, which it cannot legally add to interstate calls. Overseas, use public telephones or arrange to have calls made to you from the US. Hotel surcharges from hotels are enormous. In an emergency, call the US and have the person you're trying to reach call you right back.

TICKET-REFUND LOOPHOLE

Travel agencies pay airlines for tickets only once a week—on Tuesdays. This creates a loophole on Wednesday through Monday. If a customer needs to cancel a non-refundable ticket on one of those loophole days, the travel agency can easily void the ticket without a penalty.

Source: *The Business of Business: How 100 Businesses Really Work* by David Horowitz, Harper & Row, 10 E. 53 St., New York 10022.

COMPENSATION FOR BEING BUMPED

If you are bumped from your flight involuntarily, the airline must compensate you (with a replacement ticket and, sometimes, money) *only if* you have confirmed reservations, have met the deadline for purchasing your ticket and have checked in on time. This rule does not apply to: Charter flights. . .flights with 60 or fewer seats (which includes many commuter flights). . .inbound international flights (from a foreign country to the US). . .or when the airline reschedules the flight onto a smaller plane.

Source: Herbert J. Teison, editor, *Travel Smart*, 40 Beechdale Rd., Dobbs Ferry, New York 10522.

FOR EMERGENCIES ONLY

Most airlines waive restrictions on cheaper fares when someone must travel unexpectedly because of sudden family illness or death. And some airlines offer special "bereavement" fares. Ask the airline representative when you make reservations.

Source: Herbert J. Teison, editor, *Travel Smart*, 40 Beechdale Rd., Dobbs Ferry, New York 10522.

GET THROUGH US CUSTOMS, CHEAPLY

When you go through US customs and expect to exceed the duty-free limit for items purchased overseas, declare the most expensive items first. The lower the value of an item, the less the duty you have to pay, so you benefit by using your duty-exempt amount on the expensive items. For a list of duties imposed on popular items, write for a free copy of *Know Before You Go*, US Customs Service, Box 7118, Washington, DC 20044.

DUTY-FREE SOUVENIRS

When abroad, items worth up to $50 in local currency can be mailed into the US duty-free. And you can send each friend, relative, etc., up to $50 worth of gifts per day. Mark the package: Unsolicited gift . . . and describe the contents and value. Not exempt from duty: Alcohol, tobacco and perfume.

Source: Ed Kitridge, Public Affairs Office, US Customs Service, Washington, DC.

Car Smarts

LEGALLY IT'S A LEMON IF . . .

• Three or four repairs were attempted for the same problem . . . or

• The car was inoperable for 30 days within the first year or within 12,000 miles of the warranty period.

In both cases: The problem must substantially lower value, use or safety.

Example: Cigarette-lighter problems would not qualify, but power windows could.

To prove your car is a lemon:

• Keep accurate records of the number of repair attempts and the time the car is out of service.

• Give the dealer a dated, detailed list of problems each time you bring the car in

(and keep a copy for yourself).
• Obtain a copy of repair orders to prove when the car was not drivable.

Source: *Lemon Book: Auto Rights for New & Used Cars* by Ralph Nader and Clarence Ditlow, Moyer Bell, Ltd., Colonial Hill, Mt. Kisco, NY 10549.

BEST CAR-BUYING STRATEGY

Before even trying out the latest models:
• Determine the payments you can afford.
• Determine your "available cash."
• Do your homework.
• Shop for a car that really does fit your available cash.

Before buying the car on time. . .take the monthly payment you expect to pay on the new car and put it in your savings account for six months. See if you can handle the payments—and if you can with no problem, use what you've saved for the down payment.

Source: Credit Union National Association.

PAY LESS FOR CAR INSURANCE

Add safety features to your car and get big insurance discounts. Examples: USAA offers a 60% discount on medical and personal injury insurance for cars with air bags. Nationwide offers a 50% discount for air bags which protect all front-seat riders, a 40% discount for air bags that protect the driver only, and a 20% discount for automatic seat belts. Allstate and USAA also offer discounts on collision and liability premiums (10% and 5% respectively) for cars with four-wheel anti-lock brakes.

EXTENDED SERVICE— WASTE OF MONEY

Extended-service contracts for new cars aren't worth the extra money. The additional coverage isn't needed if the car receives proper routine maintenance. If the contract takes immediate effect, you wind up paying for coverage that's already provided free by the warranty. Some contracts require service from the dealer who sold the car.

Source: *Medical Economics*, 680 Kinderkamack Rd., Oradell, NJ 07649.

TIRE TRAP

Studies show that most automobiles have at least one tire with low air pressure, and many have two or more. Low air pressure in tires can cause poor fuel mileage and unsafe handling, as well as excessive wear and heat buildup that lead to early tire failure. Test tire pressure weekly with a dial-type gauge.

Source: *The Durability Factor*, edited by Roger P. Yepsen, Rodale Press, 33 E. Minor St., Emmaus, PA 18049.

CAR-RENTAL SCAM

Rental agents try convincing clients to upgrade reservations to larger cars because smaller ones would be "cramped and uncomfortable." When a client refuses and picks up his/her car, he may find that he was given the larger car anyway because it was the only car available.

Source: *Consumer Reports Travel Letter*, Mt. Vernon, NY 10553.